Brad Birch

Tremor

T0353372

methuen | drama

LONDON • NEW YORK • OXFORD • NEW DELHI • SYDNEY

METHUEN DRAMA
Bloomsbury Publishing Plc
50 Bedford Square, London, WC1B 3DP, UK

BLOOMSBURY, METHUEN DRAMA and the Methuen Drama logo are
trademarks of Bloomsbury Publishing Plc

First published in Great Britain 2018

A catalogue record for this book is available from the British Library.

ISBN: PB: 978-1-3500-8782-8
ePDF: 978-1-3500-8783-5
eBook: 978-1-3500-8784-2

Series: Modern Plays

Typeset by Mark Heslington Ltd, Scarborough, North Yorkshire

To find out more about our authors and books visit
www.bloomsbury.com and sign up for our *newsletters*.

TREMOR

By / Gan Brad Birch

CAST

Sophie Lisa Diveney

Tom Paul Rattray

CREATIVE TEAM / TÎM CREADIGOL

Director / Cyfarwyddwr David Mercatali

Designer / Cynllunydd Hayley Grindle

Sound Designer / Cynllunydd
Sain Sam Jones

Lighting Designer / Cynllunydd
Goleuo Ace McCarron

JMK/Sherman Assistant Director /
Cyfarwyddwr Cynorthwyol
JMK/Sherman Matthew Holmquist

Casting / Castio Nicola Reynolds

Deputy Stage Manager / Dirprwy
Rheolwr Llwyfan Kevin Smith

Assistant Stage Manager / Rheolwr
Llwyfan Cynorthwyol Emma Lang

Wardrobe Manager / Rheolwr
Gwisgoedd Deryn Tudor

Scenic Artist / Paentiwr
Golygfeydd Charlotte Neville

Set built by / Set wedi'i
hadeiladu gan Sherman Theatre
Workshops / Weithdai Theatr y Sherman

Tremor was first performed at Sherman Theatre on 12 April 2018.
Perfformiwyd *Tremor* gyntaf yn Theatr y Sherman ar 12 Ebrill 2018.

THE CREATIVE TEAM
TÎM CREADIGOL

BRAD BIRCH

Author / Awdur

Theatre includes / Theatr y cynnwys: *Black Mountain* (Paines Plough Roundabout, Edinburgh); *This Must Be the Place* (Poleroid); *En Folkefiende (An Enemy of the People)*, *The Endless Ocean* (Royal Welsh College of Music & Drama / Coleg Brenhinol Cerdd a Drama Cymru); *The Brink* (The Orange Tree); *Protest* (Old Vic); *Selfie: The Modern Day Dorian Gray* (National Youth Theatre); *Tender Bolus* (Royal Exchange Theatre & Schauspielhaus, Hamburg); *Gardening: For the Unfulfilled and Alienated* (Undeb Theatre, Edinburgh Festival & Latitude Festival – Gwobr Fringe First Award); *Milton* (Dirty Protest); *Open Court: Soap Opera, Light Arrested Between The Curtain And The Glass* (Open Court – Playwright At Your Table); *Where the Shot Rabbits Lay* (Royal Court Theatre); *Even Stillness Breathes Softly Against A Brick Wall* (Soho Theatre Upstairs); *Billy Chickens is a Psychopath Superstar* (Theatre 503, Latitude Festival).

Brad is currently under commission to the RSC, Teatro Malta, The Royal Court and he is on attachment to the National Theatre / Ar hyn o bryd mae Brad o dan gomisiwn i'r RSC, Teatro Malta, The Royal Court a dan gyswllt â'r National Theatre.

DAVID MERCATALI

Director / Cyfarwyddwr

David is Associate Director at Sherman Theatre / David yw Cyfarwyddwr Cyswllt Theatr y Sherman.

For Sherman Theatre / Ar gyfer Theatr y Sherman: *Buddy* (& Royal Welsh College of Music and Drama / Coleg Brenhinol Cerdd a Drama Cymru).

Other theatre includes / Theatr arall yn cynnwys: *Blue Heart* (Tobacco Factory Theatres & Orange Tree Theatre); *Cargo, Insignificance* (Arcola Theatre); *Radiant Vermin* (Tobacco Factory Theatres, Soho Theatre, 59E59 New York & Avignon Festival); *Tonight with Donny Stixx* (Edinburgh Fringe & The Bunker); *Little Light* (Orange Tree Theatre); *Dark Vanilla Jungle* (Edinburgh Fringe & Soho Theatre – Gwobr Fringe First Award); *Tender Napalm* (Southwark Playhouse & UK tour / taith y DU); *Every You, Every Me* (Salisbury Playhouse); *Our Ajax, Johnny got his Gun, Feathers in the Snow* (Southwark Playhouse); *Black Jesus, Coolatully* (Finborough); *Someone to Blame* (Kings Head Theatre).

HAYLEY GRINDLE

Designer / Cynllunydd

For Sherman Theatre / Ar gyfer Theatr y Sherman: *The Borrowers,
Iphigenia in Splott* (National Theatre, Schaubühne Berlin, 59E59 New
York / Efrog Newydd & UK Tour / Taith y DU), *Arabian Nights.*

Other theatre includes / Theatr arall yn cynnwys: *A Christmas Carol* (Hull Truck); *Made In
Dagenham* (Queen's Theatre Hornchurch, New Wolsey Ipswich); *Wonderman* (GaggleBabble,
National Theatre Wales & Wales Millennium Centre / Canolfan Mileniwm Cymru); *Flare
Path* (UK Tour / Taith y DU); *The Tale of Mr Tumble* (Manchester International Festival);
Little Sure Shot (Bath Theatre Royal, West Yorkshire Playhouse & Tour / Taith); *Fantastic
Mr Fox* (Singapore Repertory Theatre); *Cooking with Elvis* (Derby Theatre); *Caucasian
Chalk Circle, Britains Best Recruiting Officer* (Unicorn Theatre); *Romeo and Juliet*
(West Yorkshire Playhouse); *Mongrel Island* (Soho Theatre); *God in Ruin* (RSC).

ACE MCCARRON

Lighting Designer / Cynllunydd Goleuo

For Sherman Theatre / Ar gyfer Theatr y Sherman: *Dracula, As You Like It, Cardboard Dad,
The Almond and the Seahorse.*

Other theatre includes / Theatr arall yn cynnwys: *The Golden Dragon, Y Tŵr* (& Theatr Genedlaethol
Cymru), *Greek, The Trial* (Music Theatre Wales); *Sugar Baby* (Dirty Protest); *Of Mice and
Men* (August 012); *Cosy, Told by the Wind, The Echo Chamber* (The Llanarth Group); *Richard
Loewenherz* (Opera Magdeburg); *Newport Legends, Nightmare Scenario* (Operasonic); *The
Ecstatic Bible, Judith, The Seduction of Almighty God, Hated Nightfall* (The Wrestling School);
The Grapes of Wrath (Pitlochry Festival Theatre); *Romeo and Juliet* (National Youth Theatre
Wales / Theatr Genedlaethol Ieuenctid Cymru); *Hen Rebel, Iesu, Deffro'r Gwanwyn* (Theatr
Genedlaethol Cymru); *Gair ar Gnawd, The Tailor's Daughter* (Welsh National Opera / Opera
Cenedlathol Cymru); *The Lighthouse, Waar is Mijn Zeil?, Harawi* (Muziektheater Transparant);
The Emperor (Royal Court Theatre); *Idomeneo, La Boheme, Monster, The Devil Inside* (Scottish
Opera); *Blues for Mr Charlie* (Royal Exchange Theatre – Gwobr MEN Design Award).

SAM JONES

Sound Designer / Cynllunydd Sain

For Sherman Theatre / Ar gyfer Theatr y Sherman: *The Motherfucker with the Hat* (& Tron Theatre), *The Weir* (& Tobacco Factory Theatres), *Iphigenia in Splott* (National Theatre, Schaubühne Berlin, 59E59 New York / Efrog Newydd & UK tour / taith y DU), *Love Cardiff: City Road Stories, Arabian Nights, Home, Heritage.*

Other credits include / Credydau arall yn cynnwys: *Blackbird, St Nicholas, SAND* (The Other Room); *Richard iii Redux* (The Llanarth Group); *Looking Through Glass* (difficultlstage); *Light Waves Dark Skies, The Girl With The Incredibly Long Hair* (We Made This); *This Incredible Life* (Canoe Theatre Company); *All That I Am, Fe Ddaw'r Byd I Ben* (Richard Burton Theatre Company).

MATTHEW HOLMQUIST

JMK/Sherman Assistant Director / Cyfarwyddwr Cynorthwyol JMK/Sherman
Supported by / Cefnogwyd gan The Carne Trust

Directing credits include / Credydau fel Cyfarwyddwr yn cynnwys: *The River* (Red Oak Theatre, Loco Bristol & The Other Room); *We Had a Black Dog* (Red Oak Theatre, Theatre De Menilmontant, Paris); *See You At The End* (Theatre 503 Writer's Rapid Response, The Other Room).

Assistant Director credits include / Credydau fel Cyfarwyddwr Cynorthwyol yn cynnwys: *Simplicius Simplicissimus* (Independent Opera); *Insignificance* (Theatr Clwyd); *Kommilitonen!* (Welsh National Youth Opera / Opera Ieuenctid Cenedlaethol Cymru); *My Name is Rachel Corrie* (Graphic & The Other Room).

Associate Director credits include / Credydau fel Cyfarwyddwr Cyswllt yn cynnwys: *Le Vin Herbe, Don Giovanni* (Welsh National Opera / Opera Cenedlaethol Cymru); *A Christmas Carol* (Simply Theatre, Geneva).

CAST

LISA DIVENEY
Sophie

Theatre includes / Theatr y cynnwys: *The Seagull* (Regent's Park); *Donkey Heart* (Trafalgar Studios & Old Red Lion); *Old Vic Gala* (Old Vic); *The Hypochondriac* (Theatre Royal Bath); *Parallel Lines* (Dirty Protest); *Aristocrats, The Glass Menagerie* (Theatr Clwyd); *Moonlight, John Gabriel Borkman* (Donmar Warehouse); *A Thousand Stars Explode in the Sky* (Lyric Hammersmith); *Greta Garbo Came To Donegal* (Tricycle); *Natural Selection* (Theatre 503); *Arms and the Man* (Salisbury Playhouse); *Cleansed, Gompers* (Arcola).

TV includes / Teledu yn cynnwys: *Harlots, Grantchester, Injustice, Afterlife* (ITV); *Call the Midwife, Casualty, New Tricks, Enid, The Green Green Grass, Broken News* (BBC).

PAUL RATTRAY
Tom

For Sherman Theatre / Ar gyfer Theatr y Sherman: *Romeo and Juliet.*

Other theatre includes / Theatr arall yn cynnwys: *The Hook* (Royal & Derngate Northampton & Liverpool Everyman); *Little Light* (The Orange Tree Theatre); *Wonderland* (Hampstead Theatre); *Macbeth* (Perth & Tron Theatre); *Facts* (Dan Brodie Productions & Finborough Theatre); *Three Sisters* (Young Vic); *Racing Demon* (Sheffield Theatres Crucibles Trust); *Ditch* (High Tide Festival); *The Shawl* (Arcola Theatre); *Black Watch* (National Theatre of Scotland); *Cool Water Murder* (Belgrade Theatre); *Decky Does A Bronco* (Grid Iron Theatre); *Dinner* (National Theatre); *East Coast Chicken Supper* (Traverse Theatre); *Hand Bag* (ATC & Lyric Hammersmith); *In The Blue* (Theatre 503 & Young Vic); *The Anatomist* (Edinburgh Lyceum); *The Long and the Short and the Tall* (Crucible Theatre); *Wolfskin* (Hardware); *Shimmer* (Traverse Theatre).

TV includes / Teledu yn cynnwys: *Jamestown* (Carnival Productions); *Fortitude S.2* (Sky Atlantic & Fifty Fathoms); *Game of Thrones* (HBO & Sky Atlantic); *Holby City, Doctors, Casualty* (BBC); *Birdsong* (BBC & Working Title); *Last Rights* (Touchpaper); *Simple Things, Wet Work* (Channel 4); *The Bill* (ITV).

![Decorative bar]

WELCOME
CROESO

I am proud to have commissioned this bold and timely new play by Brad Birch.

Brad is a writer who is concerned with humanity, society and morality and he is a very exciting voice in Welsh playwriting.

Sherman Theatre is the natural home for brave new plays and I am delighted to premiere this relevant, interrogative new work in Cardiff before taking it to New York and Paines Plough's Roundabout at Theatr Clwyd and the Edinburgh Festival.

Rachel O'Riordan
Artistic Director / Cyfarwyddwr Artistig

Rwy'n falch fy 'mod wedi comisiynu'r ddrama newydd eofn ac amserol hon gan Brad Birch.

Mae Brad yn ddramodydd sydd ag affeithiad at ddynoliaeth, cymdeithas a moesoldeb ac mae'n lais hynod gyffrous ym myd y ddrama Gymreig.

Mae Theatr y Sherman yn gartref naturiol ar gyfer dramau newydd dewr ac rwyf wrth fy modd o gael dangos y gwaith newydd berthnasol, chwilfrydig hwn am y tro cyntaf yng Nghaerdydd cyn ei gymryd i Efrog Newydd a Roundabout Paines Plough yn Theatr Clwyd a Gŵyl Caeredin.

Mark Douet

CARDIFF - HOME TO THE REGIONAL THEATRE OF THE YEAR

CAERDYDD - CARTREF I THEATR RANBARTHOL Y FLWYDDYN

Based in the heart of Cardiff, Sherman Theatre is a leading producing house with a particular focus on the development and production of new work.

In January 2018 Sherman Theatre became the first in Wales to win the Regional Theatre of the Year title at The Stage Awards, recognising the Sherman as the most exciting theatre in the UK, outside of London.

Sherman Theatre makes and curates theatre for audiences in Wales, across the UK and internationally and develops the work of Welsh and Wales based artists.

Sherman Theatre generates opportunities for the citizens of Cardiff to connect with theatre through inspiring and visionary engagement.

Wedi'i lleoli yng nghanol Caerdydd, mae Theatr y Sherman yn dŷ cynhyrchu blaenllaw gyda ffocws benodol ar ddatblygu a chynhyrchu gwaith newydd.

Ym mis Ionawr 2018 Theatr y Sherman fu'r cyntaf yng Nghymru i ennill teitl Theatr Ranbarthol y Flwyddyn yng Ngwobrau The Stage, gan gydnabod y Sherman fel y theatr mwyaf cyffrous yn y DU, tu hwnt i Lundain.

Mae Theatr y Sherman yn creu a churadu theatr ar gyfer cynulleidfaoedd yng Nghymru, ar draws y DU ac yn rhyngwladol, ac yn datblygu gwaith artistiaid Cymreig a'r rheiny wedi'u lleoli yng Nghymru.

Mae Theatr y Sherman yn creu cyfleoedd i drigolion Caerdydd fedru creu cyswllt â'r theatr trwy ymrwymiad ysbrydoledig a gweledigaethol.

 029 2064 6900
shermantheatre.co.uk

 @ShermanTheatre

 Cyngor Celfyddydau Cymru
Arts Council of Wales

 Supported by
The National Lottery
through the Arts Council of Wales

 Cefnogwyd gan
Y Loteri Genedlaethol
trwy Gyngor Celfyddydau Cymru

 phf Paul Hamlyn
Foundation

Registered charity number / Rhif elusen cofrestredig 1118364

SHERMAN THEATRE STAFF LIST
RHESTR STAFF THEATR Y SHERMAN

BOARD OF TRUSTEES / YMDDIRIEDOLWYR

SHERMAN THEATR•THEATRE

❝ UNDER RACHEL O'RIORDAN'S ARTISTIC DIRECTORSHIP, THE SHERMAN HAS REVIVED ITSELF... TO BECOME A BEACON FOR NEW WRITING IN CARDIFF.❞

The Stage

EXCEPTIONAL THEATRE MADE IN CARDIFF

We take pride in creating the very best theatre for the citizens of Cardiff. Rachel O'Riordan's latest productions including *Killology* and *The Cherry Orchard* have been acclaimed by both audiences and critics alike. This acclaim has resulted in work from Wales receiving UK wide and international profile and attention. *Killology* has recently been nominated for an Olivier Award in the Outstanding Achievement in Affiliate Theatre category.

ON THE INTERNATIONAL STAGE

Sherman Theatre has proudly represented cutting edge Welsh theatre on the global stage. In Spring 2017, Sherman Theatre became the first Welsh producing house to be invited to perform at Berlin's iconic Schaubühne FIND Festival. In June 2017 we completed a hugely successful run of *Iphigenia in Splott* at New York's Brits Off Broadway Festival and look forward to returning once again this year with *Tremor*.

THEATR EITHRIADOL A WNAED YNG NGHAERDYDD

Rydym yn falch o greu'r theatr orau posibl ar gyfer dinasyddion Caerdydd. Mae cynyrchiadau diweddaraf Rachel O'Riordan gan gynnwys *Killology* a *The Cherry Orchard* wedi derbyn canmoliaeth gan gynulleidfaoedd ac adolygwyr ill dau. Mae'r ganmoliaeth wedi arwain at waith o Gymru'n derbyn sylw ac amlygrwydd trwy'r DU ac yn rhyngwladol. Enwebwyd *Killology* ar gyfer Gwobr Olivier yn ddiweddar yng nghategori Cyflawniad Eithriadol mewn Theatr Gysylltiedig.

AR Y LLWYFAN RHYNGWLADOL

Mae Theatr y Sherman wedi arddangos theatr Gymreig blaenllaw yn falch ar y llwyfan fydol. Yn ystod Gwanwyn 2017, Theatr y Sherman oedd y tŷ cynhyrchu cyntaf yng Nghymru i berfformio yng ngŵyl FIND Schaubühne yn Berlin. Yn fis Mehefin 2017 gwblhawn daith lwyddiannus iawn yn perfformio *Iphigenia in Splott* yng ngŵyl "Brits Off Broadway" Efrog Newydd ac edrychwn ymlaen at ddychwelyd unwaith eto eleni gyda *Tremor*.

NURTURING TALENT

We are committed to ensuring theatre in Wales and beyond has a strong future. We live this commitment with a range of schemes to nurture Welsh and Wales based talent. Our New Welsh Playwrights Programme connects with new writers and our regional JMK/Sherman Directors Group offers structured development for emerging directors. Both schemes are generously supported by The Carne Trust.

MEITHRIN TALENT

Rydym yn ymrwymedig i sicrhau dyfodol cryf i'r theatr yng Nghymru a thu hwnt i Gymru. Rydym yn gwireddu'r ymrwymiad hwn gydag amrywiaeth o gynlluniau i feithrin talent y Cymry a'r rhai sy'n byw yng Nghymru gan gynnwys y Rhaglen Dramodwyr Cymreig Newydd a'n Grŵp Cyfarwyddwyr JMK/Sherman rhanbarthol, a gefnogir gan The Carne Trust.

THEATRE IS FOR EVERYONE

We passionately believe that everyone should be able to enjoy the magic of theatre.

We are dedicated to providing access to great theatre for all. Our Sherman 5 scheme, which is generously supported by the Paul Hamlyn Foundation, has given many who have never had the opportunity to attend a performance at Sherman Theatre, the opportunity to do so. In addition to this work, we provide a range of opportunities for members of the community to become actively involved in our work.

In April 2017 76 members of the local community helped create *Love, Cardiff: City Road Stories*, a community play written and performed by people who live and work on Cardiff's vibrant City Road.

MAE THEATR I BAWB

Rydym yn credu'n angerddol y dylai pawb allu mwynhau hud y theatr.

Rydym yn ymroddedig i ddarparu mynediad i bawb i theatr arbennig. Mae ein cynllun Sherman 5, a gefnogir yn hael gan Sefydliad Paul Hamlyn, wedi rhoi cyfle i nifer o bobl nad oeddent erioed wedi cael y cyfle i fynychu perfformiad yn Theatr y Sherman, i wneud hynny. Yn ychwanegol at y gwaith hwn, rydym yn darparu amrywiaeth o gyfleoedd i aelodau'r gymuned ddod yn rhan weithgar o'n gwaith.

Yn fis Ebrill 2017, bu i 76 aelod o'r gymuned leol ddod ynghyd i greu *Love, Cardiff: City Road Stories*, drama gymunedol wedi'i hysgrifennu a'i berfformio gan bobl hynny sy'n byw ac yn gweithio ar hyd stryd liwgar City Road yng Nghaerdydd.

ARTIST DEVELOPMENT
DATBLYGU ARTISTIAID

We are dedicated to providing opportunities to develop and support new and emerging Welsh and Wales-based artists.

The sector can only continue to thrive and grow if creative talent is given the opportunity to benefit from the expertise of professionals in a supportive environment.

Our location in the centre of Cardiff, our position at the heart of Wales's artistic community and our links and connections with organisations across the UK mean that we are uniquely placed to nurture Welsh and Wales-based talent.

Our Artist Development schemes include:

Rydym yn ymrwymedig i gynnig cyfleoedd i ddatblygu a chefnogi artistiaid newydd a datblygol Cymreig a'r rhein sy'n byw yng Nghymru.

Gall y sector ond barhau i dyfu a ffynnu os caiff talent y cyfle i elwa o weithio mewn amgylchedd cefnogol a creadigol.

Mae ein safle yng nghanol Caerdydd, ein safle wrth wraidd cymuned artistig Cymru a'n cysylltiadau a'n cyfeillgarwch â mudiadau ar draws y DU yn golygu ein bod ni mewn safle unigryw i gefnogi talent Gymreig a'r rhai sy'n byw yng Nghymru.

Mae ein cynlluniau Datblygu Artistiaid yn cynnwys:

JMK/SHERMAN DIRECTORS GROUP
GRŴP CYFARWYDDWYR JMK

In partnership with the JMK Trust and funded by The Carne Trust our regional JMK/Sherman Directors programme develops the theatre makers of the future through workshops, discussions and paid development opportunities. Throughout 2018 a group of emerging directors will be working under the guidance of director Adele Thomas to ensure Wales is home to some of the best young directing talent.

Mewn partneriaeth â'r JMK Trust ac wedi'i noddi gan The Carne Trust, mae ein rhaglen Cyfarwyddwyr JMK/Sherman rhanbarthol yn datblygu gwneuthurwyr theatr y dyfodol trwy weithdai, trafodaethau a chyfleoedd swyddi. Trwy gydol 2018, bydd grŵp o gyfarwyddwyr sy'n dod i'r amlwg yn gweithio dan arweiniad cyfarwyddwr Adele Thomas i sicrhau bod Cymru yn gartref i rai o'r talentau cyfarwyddo ifanc gorau.

NEW WELSH PLAYWRIGHTS PROGRAMME
RHAGLEN DRAMODWYR CYMREIG NEWYDD

The 2018 New Welsh Playwrights Programme is now underway and participants will have the opportunity to develop their craft under the leadership of award-winning playwright Brad Birch. Sherman Theatre is passionate about providing a platform for Welsh and Wales based writers, ensuring the future of the arts in this country goes from strength to strength. The programme is generously supported by The Carne Trust.

Mae Rhaglen Dramodwyr Cymreig Newydd 2018 bellach ar waith a bydd y cyfranogwyr yn cael y cyfle i ddatblygu eu crefft dan fentoriaeth yr awdur gwobrwyol Brad Birch. Mae Theatr y Sherman yn frwd dros roi llwyfan i awduron Cymreig a'r rhai sy'n byw yng Nghymru, gan sicrhau bod dyfodol y celfyddydau yn y wlad hon yn mynd o nerth i nerth. Cefnogir y rhaglen yn hael gan The Carne Trust.

shermantheatre.co.uk/artist-development
shermantheatre.co.uk/datblygu-artistiaid

BE PART OF THIS CARDIFF SUCCESS STORY
BYDDWCH YN RAN O STORI LWYDDIANT CAERDYDD

BECOME A SHERMAN THEATRE BENEFACTOR

As The Stage Regional Theatre of the Year 2018, Sherman Theatre has been recognised by the industry as the most exciting theatre in the UK, outside London.

You can play a leading role in our continued success by becoming a Benefactor and supporting the creation of exceptional theatre.

An annual donation of £600* will enable us to:

- present a varied and diverse artistic programme
- reach new audiences
- engage with communities
- develop new writers and emerging artists

BYDDWCH YN GYMWYNASWR THEATR Y SHERMAN

Fel Theatr Ranbarthol y Flwyddyn The Stage yn 2018, mae Theatr y Sherman wedi'i chydnabod gan y diwydiant fel y theatr mwyaf cyffrous yn y DU, tu hwnt i Lundain.

Gallwch chwarae rhan flaenllaw yn ein llwyddiant parhaol trwy ddod yn Gymwynaswr a chefnogi'r greadigaeth o theatr eithriadol.

Gall rhodd flynyddol o £600* ein galluogi ni i:

- gyflwyno rhaglen artistig gwahanol ac amrywiaethol
- gyrraedd cynulleidfaoedd newydd
- gysylltu â chymunedau
- ddatblygu dramodwyr newydd ac artistiaid sy'n ymddangos

In addition to invitations to preview and opening performances, as a Benefactor you will have access to special events and activities where you will have the unique opportunity to experience the impact of your support first hand / Yn ychwanegol i wahoddiadau ar gyfer rhagddangosiadau a pherfformiadau agoriadol, fel Cymwynaswr fe gewch fynediad i ddigwyddiadau arbennig a gweithgareddau ble y cewch chi gyfle unigryw i brofi dylanwad eich cefnogaeth yn y cnawd.

If you would like to discuss becoming a Sherman Theatre Benefactor or for other ways to support us, please contact / Os hoffech drafod y posibiliad o fod yn Gymwynaswr Theatr y Sherman neu ffurf eraill o gefnogi, cysylltwch â:

 Emma Tropman
Fundraising Manager / Rheolwr Codi Arian
029 2064 6976

emma.tropman@shermantheatre.co.uk
shermantheatre.co.uk/support-us
shermantheatre.co.uk/cefnogi

*single payment or £50 a month over 12 months / taliad unigol neu £50 y mis dros 12 mis

Tremor

Characters

Sophie
Tom

Set

Tom's *living room.*

Modern flat-pack furniture deliberately arranged, undercut by a scattering of toddler toys.

Note on the text

(. . .) denotes speech trailing off

(/) denotes interruption

Punctuation is to suggest delivery rather than conform to the rules of grammar

Morning.

The living room.

Sophie *enters. She's wearing a jacket and carrying a bag over her shoulder.*

Tom *follows her into the room. He's in jeans and a jumper.*

Tom   Just in here.

Sophie   Nice place.

Tom   Thanks.

Sophie *puts her bag down.*

Hey look, I'm sorry about that. At the door.

Sophie   No. Don't worry.

Tom   I didn't, for a moment, I didn't recognise you. Sorry.

Sophie   No, that's alright. Understandable.

Tom   No, I should have . . . It's just, we're careful whenever we open the door, these days. Not for . . . No, that makes us sound weird, doesn't it? At the moment, we have these groups, these Christians, right. I don't know what kind they are, evangelical and I don't know what, but anyway they're different. And they're both, they both come up and down our street knocking on doors, and it's like, it seems like they're in some kind of competition with each other. And they're really going at it, really like . . . And everyone's like *argh go away*, you know? It sounds like it's nothing but it's all the time.

Sophie   Huh.

Tom   So we just, you know, we're careful, about who we open the door to. Because they'll just keep you there for ages.

Beat.

Sophie, what can I /

Sophie   / I don't mind.

Tom   What?

Sophie   I uh . . . You mean like to drink?

Tom   Oh. Um.

Sophie   You didn't mean a drink.

Tom   No, yeah. I can . . .

Sophie   No, it's alright.

Tom   I can put the kettle on.

Sophie   No, I'm sorry.

Tom   It's fine.

Sophie   I'm embarrassed now.

Tom   I was putting the kettle on anyway. Honest. It's no trouble. What is it, coffee?

Sophie   No, I don't drink coffee anymore.

Tom   A tea then? Or a cold drink?

Sophie   A tea. Thank you. Only if you're sure.

Tom   Course.

Tom *exits to the kitchen.*

Sophie *is alone in the space. She takes off her jacket.*

Her eye is drawn to a picture on the wall. It's a scribbled nest of reds and browns.

Tom *enters.*

The sound of the kettle starting to boil rises from the kitchen.

Tom *joins* **Sophie** *at the picture.*

What do you think?

Sophie   It's uh. Yeah.

Beat.

How old is . . .

Tom   Oh. Oh, no. My kid didn't do this.

Sophie   Oh.

Tom   No, we got this from IKEA.

Sophie   Oh. Sorry.

Tom   No, it's alright. I didn't pick it.

Beat.

Kettle's on anyway.

Sophie   So your, uh. Is it a boy?

Tom   Yeah.

Sophie   How old is he?

Tom   One. Well, two.

Sophie   Right.

Tom   Almost two. Yeah.

Sophie   What's he /

Tom   / George.

Sophie   Oh. George.

Tom   What's that?

Sophie   What's what?

Tom   *Oh.* Like that. What does *oh* mean?

Sophie   Did I, I didn't say oh.

Tom   You did. You said *Oh. George*.

Sophie   I didn't.

Tom   You did.

Sophie There's a royal. Isn't there? Will and Kate. Called George.

Tom Yeah.

Sophie It just, I just remembered. When you said it.

Tom Right.

Beat.

He's older. Their George.

Sophie Is he?

Tom Yeah.

The sound of the kettle clicking off.

Tom *looks off, towards the door.*

They won't be long actually. I should say. They won't, uh.

Sophie George and . . .

Tom Claire.

Sophie Right.

Tom They, they'll be home soon. Yeah.

Sophie Ok.

Tom So . . . I'll be quick. With the teas.

Sophie Don't rush.

Tom Well, no. Because if they're coming back.

Sophie I don't mind.

Tom What?

Sophie I won't be weird or anything. With them.

Tom Uh.

Sophie Try not to be anyway. You know what I'm like.

Tom I'm sorry, that's not . . .

Sophie   What?

Tom   Possible.

Sophie   Oh.

Tom   I'm sorry.

Beat.

I just, I don't think, I don't think that would be right. Too confusing.

Sophie   For George?

Tom   And Claire. In a way. Too. Not confusing. Weird.

Sophie   I said I won't be weird.

Tom   The situation.

Beat.

Sophie   Does she know?

Tom   Course she does.

Sophie   You told her?

Tom   Why wouldn't I?

Sophie   No, I just. I wondered.

Tom   I wouldn't lie.

Sophie   I didn't mean it to sound like you'd lie.

Tom   Then why did you ask?

Sophie   Because it's sometimes easier. Isn't it? To just not say. And not saying isn't the same thing as lying. It's . . .

Tom   What?

Sophie   Keeping things in the past.

Beat.

Tom   Well I didn't with her.

Sophie   No.

Tom   And even so, even though she . . . I just don't think this, unannounced. Unplanned. I don't think it's a good idea.

Sophie   Ok.

Tom   We've been having a . . . It's just not the right time.

Sophie   You don't have to explain.

Tom   I'm not. I'm just saying.

Tom *glances at his watch*.

Hey, you know what, why don't we . . . Maybe it's better if we just, if we went out for something.

Sophie   Out?

Tom   There's a café round the corner. It's alright. They're nice people there. We go there, been there, a bit.

Sophie   You and Claire?

Tom   Yeah. When we can.

Sophie   What do you reckon they'd make of this?

Tom   Of what?

Sophie   You turning up with another woman?

Tom   It's not like that.

Sophie   I know it isn't.

Tom   They're nice people.

Sophie   Nice people gossip, don't they?

Tom   They know me.

Sophie   Exactly.

Tom   What?

Sophie   Oh, I'm joking.

Tom   I didn't even think of being /

Sophie   / I'm messing around.

Tom   Then don't. Please.

Sophie   Alright. Sorry.

Beat.

I'm sorry, Tom. That was inappropriate. I didn't mean to /

Tom   / It's alright.

Sophie   I'll just . . .

Sophie *picks up her bag and jacket.*

Tom   Wait. What are you doing?

Sophie   I thought we were going to the café.

Tom   We're not going to the café now.

Sophie   What?

Tom   No, I don't think that'll be a good idea at all.

Sophie   Because of what I said?

Tom   I've got to live around here, Sophie. You can't take the piss.

Sophie   I'm not taking the piss. It was a joke. I knew it was wrong the moment I said it. I'm sorry. I'm nervous. We haven't seen each other in /

Tom   / Four years.

Sophie   Yeah.

Tom   About four.

Tom *looks out the window.*

Sophie   Where did they go?

Tom   What?

Sophie   Claire and George. Where are they?

Tom   They just . . . To pick up a present.

Sophie   For you?

Tom   For George's friend. It's his birthday tomorrow and we need to take him something. Not his friend. They're like, they're our friends. His parents. Not that they don't, they get on and everything. It's just, at that age they don't really have the ability.

Sophie   Ability?

Tom   To be like, friends in the way we mean. They can play with the same toys and that, but they're not really, uh, interacting in the, with each other like . . . Am I making sense?

Sophie   Yeah.

Tom   Am I?

Sophie   Yeah.

Beat.

Tom   Look. Let's have these teas, we can have a, then uh . . .

Sophie   Sure.

Tom   But we'll have to be quick.

Sophie   Yeah. Ok.

Tom *exits.*

Sophie *goes to the window. She spots something. She smiles and raises her hand to wave.*

Tom *returns with two mugs of tea.*

He puts them down. She turns.

Sophie   Thanks.

Tom   Kettle was still warm, so it should be, will be alright to drink. What are you looking at?

Sophie   There was a boy.

Tom   Oh right.

Sophie   Playing, on his bike.

Tom   That's, uh, that's probably Michael.

Sophie   Do you know him?

Tom   Oh yeah. He's Harriet and Rob's kid. He doesn't go to the normal school so he just hangs around the streets some days.

Sophie   What do you mean he doesn't go to normal school?

Tom   Well he's an idiot. He can't get on in normal classes.

Sophie   Right.

Tom   Sorry, I don't mean idiot.

Sophie   It's ok.

Tom   Special, is what I meant. He's special needs.

Sophie   I know what you meant.

Beat.

Tom   You were always on top of that. My language.

Sophie   What do you mean?

Tom   Saying the wrong thing.

Sophie   Makes it sound like I was telling you off.

Tom   No. Just like, you knew, didn't you? You know what, he's a good kid. He's alright, Michael. Expert on the football. Ask him anything about the league and he'll tell you. Ask him which bloody player sneezed on the fourth of whenever and he'll be able to tell you.

Sophie *turns back to the window.*

Sophie   It's a nice area, Tom. You've done alright.

Tom   It can be. There's a train station just down the road and sometimes people, people sometimes park up on our street if the carpark there overflows. Pain in the arse that. You've got all these, don't know who they are, parking up and down the road all day.

Sophie   Looks alright today.

Tom   Yeah, today's alright but it's not always like this. You'll have to believe me.

Sophie   I do.

Tom   Going to make me sound paranoid.

Beat.

Are you still in the same place yourself then?

Sophie   Yeah. Same flat.

Tom   Right.

Sophie   Different landlord now though.

Tom   Is it?

Sophie   Yeah. So, Mr Timms. You remember him?

Tom   Yeah, yeah, course. With the comb-over and the yellow jumper.

Sophie   Oh god, that jumper.

Tom   And the smell, that smell always coming through his door.

Sophie   Bacon.

Tom   That was bacon, was it? Christ. The state them pigs must've been in to stink like that.

Sophie   Yeah.

Tom   So what happened, did he die or what?

Sophie   Oh no. He's not dead. No, he just sold up. Moved away.

Tom   Oh right.

Sophie   Moved back to where his, living near his kids now, I think.

Tom   Right. Had kids, did he?

Sophie   It's a Mr Choudhury now.

Tom   Is it? Nice, is he?

Sophie   He's alright. Seems alright. He doesn't live downstairs, rents that out too, so that's something. And he let me paint the place, so.

Tom   Right.

Sophie   I don't, actually, I don't know him that well.

Tom   You never really do. Landlords, I mean.

Beat.

Sophie   So what made you come here?

Tom   Oh well, uh. We wanted to buy. And Claire's family's from here. So it's handy for the childcare and that.

Sophie   Is Claire money then?

Tom   Is she what?

Sophie   Is she money, come from money? Buying round here.

Tom   Oh. Her parents helped, they're teachers.

Sophie   Landed on your feet then, haven't you?

Tom   Yeah well, we get by.

Sophie   Quick, to have George.

Tom   What?

Sophie   To have a two-year-old.

Tom   Almost two.

Sophie   From scratch, yeah.

Tom   It's what we wanted.

Sophie   I never thought you were the type.

Tom   For what?

Sophie   Kids.

Tom   Why not?

Sophie   I don't know.

Tom   I like kids.

Sophie   Do you?

Tom   Yeah. I've always . . . We just never spoke about it. It's not a conversation we had.

Sophie   No.

Tom   Do you have kids?

Sophie   No. Fuck no.

Tom   Right.

Beat.

So what are you doing? Are you working at the same place?

Sophie   No. Left that. I'm at a, same thing, I'm still on the phones, just at somewhere else now.

Tom   Right.

Sophie   Money's the same. But when it's quiet I get to check on eBay and that. So.

Tom   That's something then.

Sophie   Yeah. Suppose it is.

Tom   Suppose?

Sophie   Not what I want to be doing forever. Feels like I've already been doing it forever, but still.

Tom   Yeah. No, I get that.

Sophie   Trying to get out there, trying to do more stuff.

Tom   Well, good. That's good.

Sophie   So what about, what do you do then, these days? Do you work in town?

Tom   Ah, I work from home.

Sophie   Oh. Right.

Tom   It's a new business.

Sophie   Your business?

Tom   Yeah, it's just . . . It's not going to change the world or nothing. Not going to make me a millionaire. But I'm my own boss.

Sophie   What is it you do?

Tom   Well it's just selling stuff, really. Bits and pieces. Kettles, food processors, at the moment. It's all on Amazon and that.

Sophie   You sell kettles?

Tom   Yeah, like, now because they're cheap. Last month it was yoga mats. I don't see any of it. It's just all in these big warehouses in China and the stuff gets delivered to the customer. Like I said, it's pennies, what I get. I'm just sat on the internet all day, really. The office parties are a bit shit.

Sophie   Yeah, I bet.

Tom   Should be working now actually.

Sophie   Oh sorry. I've just turned up.

Tom   No, it's fine. Besides, if I wasn't here then there'd have been no one to answer the door.

Sophie   Yeah. Or I could have bumped into Claire.

Beat.

Don't worry, I'd have made something up. I wouldn't have, you know.

Tom   Wouldn't have what?

Sophie   Well I wouldn't just, you know, this is your life.

Tom   I haven't kept anything from her. I don't know why you think I'd hide it.

Sophie   No. I don't mean that. I'm just trying to be respectful.

Tom   We don't keep anything from each other.

Sophie   Well that's good.

Tom   It's more that I haven't planned it, it isn't planned.

Sophie   No. I know. I get it.

Pause.

Tom   How long are you in town for?

Sophie   Just the day.

Tom   That's a way to come, just the day. What did you come here for?

Sophie   To see you.

Beat.

Tom   Are you joking?

Sophie   No.

Tom   Hang on. That's . . . I don't understand.

Sophie   I need to talk to you about something.

Tom   You get the train all this way to, to . . .

Sophie   I drove. I've got a car now, actually. Learnt to drive. Like I said. Getting out there.

Tom   Sophie /

Sophie *points out the window.*

Sophie   / You can see it there. The red Focus.

Tom   Sophie, what the hell? How did you even . . .

Sophie   Sorry.

Tom   What are you sorry for?

Sophie   The shock of it. I can understand it's a shock. Your face when you opened the door.

Tom   No, that was just /

Sophie   / It's ok. I'm not taking offence.

Beat.

I emailed you. I did try. I emailed you a couple of times. Asking to speak to you.

Tom   I didn't get any emails.

Sophie   No. I didn't get a reply.

Tom   I've a different address now.

Sophie   I hoped so, yeah.

Tom   Hoped?

Sophie   That you weren't just ignoring me.

Beat.

Tom   What if I was?

Sophie   What?

Tom   What if I was and I didn't want to talk and you've just turned up anyway?

Sophie   I thought about that. Thought about that a lot, actually. But then I thought. No. Not replying isn't saying no.

Tom   It could be, in a way.

Sophie   In a way?

Tom   As a gesture.

Sophie   So you did get them then?

Tom   No. I'm just saying.

Beat.

How did you, I mean, to find me, where I live. How did you even get my address?

Sophie   I just asked around.

Tom   Around?

Sophie   A friend gave it to me.

Tom   Who?

Beat.

Who gave it to you, Sophie?

Sophie   I don't want to say.

Tom   Why not?

Sophie   You'll be pissed off with them and they were just doing me a favour.

Tom   Gavin.

Sophie   Tom, I'm not going to /

Tom   / It was Gav, wasn't it?

Sophie   No.

Tom   Christ.

Sophie   Tom.

Tom   You know he always liked you. Fancied you. You know that, don't you?

Sophie   No he didn't.

Tom   He fucking did. He was always like . . . It's why he was always like he was when we'd be out. Putting me down and that. Didn't you notice?

Sophie   He wouldn't put you down.

Tom   He'd do it all the time. Little comments.

Sophie   That's just how you were with each other. You were just as bad.

Tom   Come on. You knew he liked you. That's why you asked him.

Sophie   It was Rob Allen who told me.

Tom   Rob Allen?

Sophie   Yeah.

Tom   Why did he give it to you? He wouldn't just . . .

Sophie   I know his girlfriend. Hannah. I asked her to ask him where you lived now.

Tom   To give to you?

Sophie   Yeah. No. Well, I don't know.

Tom   You don't know? What does that mean?

Sophie   I mean I just asked her. I don't know if she told him who it was for.

Tom   Fucking hell.

Sophie   So don't /

Tom   / Fucking hell, Sophie.

Sophie   It's not his fault.

Pause.

Tom   I haven't spoken to him in, what, a year.

Sophie   Hannah said he wasn't sure how you were doing.

Beat.

Do you chat to anyone? From home.

Tom   This is my home.

Sophie   I mean Wrexham.

Tom   No. It's cleaner, clearer to not. To draw a line. This is the person I am now. It's the person I want to be, should have been for a long time. I was in a sad place. Things got dark, and I . . . I'm better now. I'm in a better place.

Beat.

Who would you have said you were, if it was Claire who answered the door?

Sophie   I thought you said she knows.

Tom   But you didn't know that, when you rang the bell. What were you going to say?

Sophie   Why does it matter?

Tom   It just does.

Sophie   I'd have probably said I was an old school friend or something. I don't know.

Tom   You don't know?

Sophie   I hadn't really thought.

Tom   No.

Beat.

Well it's a good job it was me who got you then.

Sophie   I didn't expect I'd be such a problem.

Tom   What did you expect?

Pause.

Sophie   What did you tell her?

Tom   I just told her what happened. That I was involved in an accident. That a bus drove off a bridge and killed a lot of people. That there weren't many survivors.

Sophie   Right.

Tom   And I told her that I was in a relationship. When it happened. That we were both involved.

Sophie   What did she say?

Tom *looks out the window.*

Tom   Is that why you're here?

Sophie   What?

Tom   Me and Claire. Asking questions about her.

Sophie   No. I'm just asking. I'm just, I'm asking about your life . . . I don't want it to be awkward.

Tom   She'd heard of the crash. She remembered seeing it on the news.

Sophie   Right.

Tom   And the court case. She followed it a bit. I suppose people did.

Sophie   Did she recognise you?

Tom   No.

Sophie   Do you believe that?

Beat.

Tom   She asked why we split up.

Sophie   Brave question.

Tom   I've got nothing to be ashamed of.

Sophie Did you tell her the truth?

Tom Most of it.

Sophie Most?

Tom I told her my side of it.

Beat.

What do you do? When you're with people. Do you tell them?

Sophie It's simpler to not. It's not like I lie or anything. It's just, you find a way of making sure it never comes up.

Tom You keep it in the past.

Sophie Yeah.

Beat.

Tom Look. I'm sorry about the door and the Rob Allen thing. You're not a problem, I just . . . Claire and George will be back any minute and then we've got to take this present to this house. I'm just, it's not unreasonable to have things to do. You just turned up.

Sophie The birthday's tomorrow.

Tom What?

Sophie You said the kid's birthday's tomorrow.

Tom We're taking the present today.

Pause.

Sophie Did you change your email address so I couldn't find you?

Tom Find me?

Sophie Contact you.

Tom We haven't spoken in years.

Sophie So it was working?

Tom   It was a, I wanted a fresh start. Needed a fresh start. I'm allowed that. I'm allowed to do that, I can change my email address if I . . . It had nothing to do with you.

Beat.

Sophie   Why did you make the tea?

Tom   What?

Sophie   If you don't have time to talk to me, why didn't you just stop me at the door?

Tom   Because I wanted to make sure you were ok.

Sophie   Ok?

Tom   That you weren't in trouble.

Sophie   Trouble?

Tom   Yeah, like . . .

Sophie   Wanted to make sure I wasn't after a kidney or whatever. That I didn't have a three-year-old waiting in the car with your name on.

Tom   Don't. I don't mean that.

Sophie   What kind of trouble do you mean?

Tom   Not trouble like that. I was concerned. You know, you just turn up at my door, I don't know how you've found me.

Sophie   Ah.

Tom   What?

Sophie   So that's it.

Tom   What's it? What are you talking about?

Sophie   The trouble you mean. It's trouble for you. Not me. You needed to find out if you were ok.

Tom   No.

Sophie   Why didn't you just say that? That's something you've always done.

Tom   What?

Sophie   Masking what you're really thinking, what you're really after with this, kind of, fake care. You don't have to pretend, Tom. You should just say it.

Tom   Well I am saying. I'm saying it now. I was fucking shocked.

Sophie   And angry.

Tom   No. No, I wasn't /

Sophie   / That this wasn't in your control.

Tom   I'm allowed to protect my own home.

Sophie   Protect? Like you're under attack?

Tom   Yeah. This feels a bit like an attack right now, yeah.

Beat.

Sophie   I'm sorry. I didn't mean for /

Tom   / What the hell are you doing here, Sophie? Why are you here now?

Sophie   The driver. Of the bus. He's dying. He's in hospital, and he's dying.

Beat.

Tom   Right.

Sophie   It's cancer. He's had it a long time. But this is it, they think it'll be weeks. Days, even.

Tom   Huh.

Tom *circles the room. He ends up back where he was.*

Well thanks for telling me.

Sophie   Thanks?

Tom   Yeah.

Sophie   *Thanks*.

Tom   What did you, you can't expect me to just have an instant reaction to something like that. I don't, I mean what, do you want me to say I'm sorry or something?

Sophie   No.

Tom   I haven't even thought about the guy for . . .

Beat.

How did you find out?

Sophie   He told me.

Tom   He, you've spoken to him?

Sophie   Yeah.

Tom   Why the hell were you speaking to him, Sophie?

Sophie   Because he asked to talk. He wrote to me and asked me to come to the hospital.

Tom   And you went?

Beat.

Sophie, what the hell?

Sophie   It wasn't easy to go. But I'm glad I did. I almost missed it, the letter. I don't really pay attention to letters anymore. All that ever comes is just bills and junk and I just let it all pile up in the hall, and if it's anything important then they'll find a way of getting in touch. So this, it just sat there, with the rest of it, and I'm about to throw it all out, and I notice this . . . It had a handwritten address, and a postmark from the hospital. I thought *what the hell is this?* I open it, and I read the first line. *Sophie Bufton. While I can imagine this letter will come as a shock, I hope it doesn't upset you.* And I stop. I know exactly who it is, I knew it was him. And I put the letter down and I leave it. A day, two days. It's not

that I didn't want to read it. I knew I would. I just couldn't.
Yet. See, I'd done a lot, trying to get myself together. I'd just
got this new job. And I'd learnt to drive, and my cousin was
selling his car and even though it was a pile of shit, it was
cheap and I could afford it. So I had this new job and a new
car and a bit of fucking . . . determined that this, now I'll be
able to break out of this cycle. Except none of it actually did
anything. The job was just the old job but with different
paint on the walls, and while I bought a car, I had nowhere
to drive it. So here I was, a few days, a week, two weeks down
the line, and I was exactly where I've always been. And all
the while, this letter sat there. I'd actually been thinking
about him. Not on purpose, and not even about the crash
itself, I just sometimes found myself wondering about him.
As a person. And getting this letter felt, it felt unreal. As
though I'd summoned him, as though my thinking about
him caused him to write. That he knew in some way. It
sounds weird. But it sounds even weirder, the idea that we'd
both just been thinking about each other, completely
separately, at the same time. So one night, after work, I go
home and I make a cup of tea and I pick up the letter and I
read it, all. In it, he tells me he's dying, that he has cancer
and that while he was fighting it, it had spread across his
body and they couldn't catch up with it. He says that he
doesn't think he has long and that he wants to talk. In
person. With me. With us. He thought we were still together.
And I put the letter down and breathed out, for what must
have been the first breath since I started reading it. I
couldn't do it. I thought I couldn't, knew I couldn't. I could
barely convince myself to get out of bed every morning.
Each day up and out being a massive fucking achievement in
my eyes. What on earth he'd want from me, and how I'd
even manage to get there, I had no idea. And so I slept on it.
Or, well, no. I didn't sleep. I couldn't. I laid there in bed,
awake, for days now, I miss some time off work, fake a
sickness on the phone, and commit to being indoors. Stuck
there and wondering, thinking to myself. *Ok. If I can't do this,
then what can I do? What would I get up for? Work? No. I'd rather*

lose the job. Would I get up if my flat was burning down? Yes. Ok.
That's one thing. If my mum . . . And so on. And this, I thought
of him, sat there, why he'd want to, need to write to me. And
I thought *well if I can do anything, I can drive my car and go to*
the hospital.

Beat.

I didn't know what to expect. I was sat in the carpark for
fucking ages. I smoked three cigarettes, one after the other. I
almost didn't go. I almost just drove straight out again, but
I'd already got the parking ticket. I'd got the little ticket and
thought *well you've committed now.* It's funny, the things you
. . . And I went in, and I asked for him and I found his ward
and was taken to his bed. And he was just sat there. He wrote
a number on the letter, but I didn't call it, I just went, so he
wasn't expecting me. And so when he saw me, it wasn't just
shock, it was fear. Automatic fear. He told me after, that he
has panic attacks, that he has quite bad panic attacks, and
he'd just recovered from one just before I arrived. I told him
I'd been in the car park for twenty minutes and he was glad
that I'd waited. I told him I have anxiety too, that it's there,
just under the surface, all the time. And the weirdest stuff
can trigger it. He asked me if it was tough getting his letter
and I told him that it was. He thought I'd ignored it or
ripped it up, or. Just the other day, he said, he'd written off
ever thinking that I'd get in touch. That I wasn't going to
come and that it was wrong of him to have tried to get in
touch with me. He worried that he'd hurt me. But I told him
that he hadn't, that I just needed time. And he was relieved,
more than that, happy. And we spoke for about half hour.
He told me about his cancer. He was quite matter of fact
about it. I found it more uncomfortable than he did. And
then at the end, before I left, he asked me. He asked me to
forgive him. And he asked me to ask you to forgive him too.
And I promised that I would.

Tom   Why? Why did you promise that, Sophie?

Sophie   Because I feel, I felt guilty. In a way.

Tom   We did nothing wrong.

Sophie   That's not true.

Beat.

Tom   Look. I can't imagine what it must be like to get a letter like that. He shouldn't have done it. He shouldn't have put you in that position. But I'm sorry, I won't have any part of it.

Sophie   You should have seen him, Tom. He needs this.

Tom   I don't care what he needs. Thirty-two people died because of him. He crashed that bus, Sophie. By rights, he should be dead too.

Sophie   Tom /

Tom   / And just because we survived, it doesn't mean we're not victims either. We survived him, and he's writing letters and . . . No. Maybe you're ok with that, you do what you want. But not me. Not this. Not today.

Beat.

You know what, I think it's better if you just go.

Sophie   Tom.

Tom   Leave. Please. Will you?

Sophie *gathers her things.*

Sophie   I'm sorry. I didn't mean to upset you.

Sophie *goes to leave.*

Tom   Do you know how hard it's been to start again like this? To start from scratch, build a life, build a family, knowing full well what can happen, what happens in this world, and to have faith in it again?

Sophie   Yes, Tom. I do. Fuck. Of course I do.

Sophie *goes to leave again.*

Tom   I'm sorry. I know. I didn't mean . . . I sometimes snap, I sometimes . . . I lose my temper because I struggle. I struggle to talk about this.

Sophie   Yeah.

Tom   I'm sorry.

Sophie   I . . . I remember, a few months after the crash, Mr Timms told me that when he saw it on the news, that they said that no survivors were expected. Not one. And yet there were seven of us. Seven people in the world did something that day that they shouldn't have. They lived. That's insane, Tom. Of course we struggle.

Tom   You have to make things make sense.

Sophie   Yes.

Tom   And I can't make sense of doing anything for that man. Sentenced for seven years. Served two. Two years he spent in prison, for thirty-two deaths. Now, I don't believe in nothing spiritual. You know that. But this. The idea that he's sat there in that condition now. That's justice. I used to get worried that, when George would be old enough to start asking questions, I worried that I wouldn't be able to tell him, explain to him, properly, the difference between right and wrong. Because I didn't believe in any distinction anymore. Because I'd seen bad things go unpunished, and I'd seen good deeds go ignored. But this is a sign. I don't feel sorry for that man, Sophie. I'm relieved.

Sophie   I think whatever you feel about him, whatever anger you feel, whatever hate, whatever pain or torture or harm you wish on him, he feels and wishes it on himself more. He spoke about that, he's convinced that this isn't just cancer. It's bigger than that. It's /

/ **Tom**'s *mobile rings.*

Tom *turns away to answer the call.*

(*On phone.*) Uh, hi darling. How are you doing? Yeah, yeah. I'm alright. What's the matter? Oh really?

Tom *checks his watch.*

Right ok.

Tom *turns to* **Sophie**, *then turns away.*

Well you do what you think. Yeah. Ok. Bye. Yeah, love you.

Tom *hangs up.*

Beat.

Sophie   Everything alright?

Tom   They've gone to drop the present off.

Sophie   Right.

Beat.

Tom   You know, I've got to tell you, Sophie. I can't believe this. After four years of nothing, you travel all this way because some stranger, worse than a stranger, less than a stranger, because someone who almost killed you, asked for, for your forgiveness. It makes no sense.

Sophie   I've tried to explain.

Tom   No, you've explained your part well enough. It's him, it's him I don't understand.

Sophie   Would you like to speak to him yourself?

Tom   No. No, I wouldn't, Sophie. It's not forgiveness that he wants. It's pity. And you, going to him, entertaining this, you're giving him exactly what he wants.

Sophie   I don't pity him. It's not pity. No, it was heavier than that. I felt a weight in my heart by how small he was. And everyone there, the nurses, the doctors, the porters. They were waiting for him to give up. Give up so that the next person could take the bed. That's not life. He's already dead.

Tom   Well better that than being wiped out in an instant.

Sophie   I don't know.

Tom   Sophie.

Sophie   There's something in not knowing. There's something in living your life right through to the last second, don't you think?

Tom   What so he, so he did those people a favour?

Sophie   No. I'm not saying that.

Tom   He wasted those lives.

Sophie   I don't mean that, I mean /

Tom   / He's a murderer.

Sophie   It wasn't murder.

Tom   It's the same thing.

Sophie   No it isn't.

Tom   What's the difference?

Sophie   There's a lot of difference, Tom.

Tom   Not for the victims.

Sophie   Who says?

Tom   Us, Sophie. We're victims too.

Sophie   You can't speak for the dead.

Tom   But you can imagine. You can imagine which side they'd be on. Ours. Not his.

Sophie   Do you think, if they had the choice, do you think they'd rather be us? Do you think compared to what they are now, do you think they'd rather be here, doing this, me and you?

Tom   Are you comparing my life to being dead?

Sophie   No, I'm just saying, we can't presume to know what kind of lives people would want. That people would be happy with.

Tom   So some people would rather be dead than be me?

Sophie   No, I'm not saying that.

Tom   So what are you saying?

Sophie   I just think you need to /

Tom   / Or maybe, maybe. I don't need to do anything. Maybe I'm fine the way I am. Maybe I'm fine believing what I believe, and coping the way I cope, and you're fine with whatever you're doing. What has this got to do with you? I'm living my life. I didn't ask you to come here.

Beat.

Sophie   So is this, what you've got here, is this what you wanted?

Tom   What?

Sophie   When you were younger. This. Is this what you had in mind? Owning a flat. A kid. Your own business. Christians knocking on your door.

Tom   Don't take the piss.

Sophie   I'm not taking the piss.

Tom   I've worked hard for this.

Sophie   And I can tell. I'm just asking why. Is this what you wanted, Tom? Or have you learned to want it?

Tom   I'm proud of what I've done.

Beat.

Sophie   You used to take the piss.

Tom   What?

Sophie   You say *don't take the piss*. But you used to take the piss all the time.

Tom   When?

Sophie   All the time. At everything. When that pub in Brynteg turned into a restaurant and then closed. When Matt and Simon came out as a couple. When Carys took that French course at the college.

Tom   Yeah well what the fuck did Carys need French for?

Sophie   When anyone did anything. Now look at you. What do you reckon you'd have said about this?

Tom *looks out the window.*

Tom   That person, that's not me. Whoever that was, that's not me anymore.

Sophie   Because you live in a nice town?

Tom   No. Because of in here. *(Taps the side of his head.)* Sure, I might have taken the piss a lot. But that's because I didn't know any better. It's because I never had anything of my own. And I was lonely, and confused, and frustrated. My life is different now, so I'm different. Why's that so hard for you to understand? I mean what, are you telling me you're the same person as you was then? What did you want? When you were younger, did you see yourself having to give yourself reasons to get up in the morning? Was this what you had in mind?

Sophie   No.

Tom   No.

Sophie   By now I thought we'd be living on the moon.

Pause.

Tom   Look. Why didn't you just, what does it matter what I actually think? He'll never know, he'll never find out. He's what, days, weeks away from dying, you say? Why didn't you just lie to him instead of coming all this way?

Sophie   I thought of that. Of doing that. I was ready to call him and say that I'd been to see you and though it was hard, you eventually said yes. And he'd have thanked me, thanked you, and that would be that. The end of it. But then I thought no. Because what if you actually did want to forgive him, what if you needed this too.

Beat.

I forgive him. He asked me and I answered right away. I felt it and I thought it, and I do. I forgive him, Tom.

Tom   I know you do.

Sophie   You know?

Tom   Come on. It was never in doubt. From day one of the inquiry, you supported him.

Sophie   Supported?

Tom   Absolutely.

Sophie   There's a difference between supporting someone and saying that more could have been done.

Tom   Yeah. More could have been done. Like stopping him from being on the fucking road in the first place.

Sophie   Like the company taking responsibility for the working conditions of the drivers. Like the government stopping them from forcing people to work unrealistic timetables, cutting breaks and time off.

Tom   Sophie.

Sophie   But no. None of that. No one was held accountable, no one apologised, no one lost their job. Because they had their man.

Tom   He was driving the bus, Sophie.

Sophie   He was also Muslim.

Beat.

Tom   Look. I'm not going back over that.

Sophie   He was made a scapegoat by the press, by the company and by the court.

Tom   It had nothing to do with /

Sophie   / It had everything to do with /

Tom   / The inquiry concluded it was his fault. And you can call it whatever you like, that's the law.

Sophie   The police were desperate. The way they put pressure on us to /

Tom   / There wasn't any pressure.

Sophie   Telling us that inquiries go on forever, that nothing might come of it. That all those people would have died and nothing would happen. They said that to me, Tom. So I know they said it to you. They asked you to /

Tom   / To tell the truth. I told them what I knew.

Sophie   You told them you could smell alcohol.

Tom   Yes.

Sophie   That when you paid for your ticket, as he lent forward, you could smell it on his breath.

Tom   That's what I said.

Sophie   A fact that you didn't mention to me on the bus, that you didn't mention on the day, for a week. Not until the third statement do you say that you thought that you smelled drink on the driver. Why didn't you say it before, Tom? Why did you never say it to me?

Tom   I don't remember. Maybe I did.

Sophie   No. You didn't. I so wish you did. I sit and I try and convince myself that you did but you didn't.

Tom   There was a lot going on. I can't explain how memories work. Christ, Sophie. We were in shock.

Sophie   It wasn't shock.

Tom   Then what? I wasn't lying. The blood tests proved it. He'd been drinking. What did I do? Slip a pint into him while he was in a coma? Or was it a lucky guess?

Sophie   In court, the lead DI said that they couldn't say for certain that there was enough in his bloodstream to impair his driving, they couldn't rule out that the traces could have been from that morning or the night before. The test alone couldn't prove it.

Tom   That test was compromised. They took too long getting the sample. That's all that was.

Sophie   So your testimony put it all together. They came to you because you were the only surviving passenger whose conversation with the driver remained on the CCTV. They came to you because you were the only one. What did they say to you in that third interview, Tom? What did they tell you to say?

Tom   What I knew. The truth.

Beat.

Sophie   There was something different about you. I remember it so clearly.

Tom   What do you mean?

Sophie   After the third interview. You called me as you left, asking if I wanted you to come and visit me on the ward. And I remember hearing, hearing something in your voice. I asked you how it went, and you said that it went really well. And I wondered what you meant.

Tom   Look. They, it was stressful. Having to go through the day, exactly what happened, over and over.

Sophie   I couldn't understand it. I couldn't understand why they kept interviewing you.

Tom   I was the only one who'd been discharged.

Sophie   No. No, it was more than that.

Tom   What then? Why me, Sophie? What was it about me?

Sophie   You enjoyed it. The attention. The way the police spoke to you.

Tom   Sophie.

Sophie   You told me once. Do you remember? You told me how, when you left school, you applied to join the police. You did, didn't you?

Tom   What's that got to do with . . .

Sophie   You couldn't wait. You coasted through the end of school and went straight to recruitment.

Tom   Kids. When you're a kid you just apply for everything.

Sophie   And the exams and stuff, that they make you do. You failed them. And not by a few marks, you'd properly failed them. It broke your heart, Tom. I remember you telling me.

Tom   That's got, it's got nothing to do with /

Sophie   / And so when this happens, when they come up to you, and they're nice to you, friendly with you. You liked it. You wanted to be a part of it.

Tom   I wanted to do the right thing.

Sophie   They played you. They knew exactly how to play you. Make you feel like one of the boys, tell you how hard, how difficult it is to get straightforward stuff done, and then they asked you for a favour.

Tom   No.

Sophie   Say that you could tell the driver was drunk. Put it beyond doubt.

Tom   No, Sophie.

Sophie   Because after all, they found the booze in his blood, it's not like he hadn't had a drink.

Tom   Stop it.

Sophie   What does it matter if it was the night before?

Tom   Stop it. Stop it, Sophie. Christ.

Sophie   Besides, if they'd have got the bloods earlier, they'd have shown, clearly. It was red tape, red tape getting in the way of justice. *You know how it is, don't you, mate?*

Tom   Enough.

Sophie   I don't blame you, Tom. I don't. We were in a vulnerable place and they knew exactly how to play you, how to take advantage.

Beat.

It's ok to feel annoyed with that.

Beat.

You came to see me. That night. You came to the ward. You brought crisps. We watched the news together on the TV. We watched the report, they were filming from outside the hospital, we could have waved from the window. And they said that they had arrested the driver. And I knew it was you. What we'd been through. I'd have wanted to be useful too. I just wish you spoke to me about it first.

Tom   What does that mean? What does that mean, Sophie?

Sophie   I mean I wish we'd have had chance to chat, before /

Tom   / If I'd have come to you, lying in that bed, with your broken arm and fractured shoulder, and I told you that I thought the driver was drunk, would you have told me to not say?

Sophie   I'd have asked you exactly what you remember happening.

Tom   That's what they did.

Sophie   I'd have asked you why you didn't say anything as we got on the bus.

Tom   They asked me that too.

Sophie   I'd have said to you Tom, *Jesus Christ, do you realise what you're saying here?* I'd have asked you why you thought they might have been telling us that inquiries mean fuck all gets done. I'd have asked you what you think they might have wanted you to say. And I'd have asked you to think carefully about the consequences in case you were wrong.

Tom   Sophie, I thought about that. All of that.

Sophie   And I'd have asked you, Tom, who you'd think would have welcomed the news that it was the Muslim driver to blame.

Beat.

It didn't take them a second. I remember thinking, thinking how the hell, how they hell do they make those boards so quickly. Do you know what I mean? The boards and banners they had with them, outside the court.

Tom   Yes, Sophie. Yes I do.

Sophie   Do they just have lots of card and pens and that about, or do they go and quickly buy a load once they hear about a story on the news? Do you reckon they know at WH Smith when people are buying craft stuff to make racist signs?

Tom   What have those nutter groups got to do with us? With this? They don't matter, they never mattered.

Sophie   Because it wasn't just the racists, Tom. It was the papers too. They all went for it. You gave them something and they jumped on it. A chance to speculate on whether more Muslims were going to drive more buses off the road.

Tom   That started, that all started, when they found booze in his blood. No, it started before that, when he had a drink before he started his shift.

Beat.

Sophie   You know, he spoke about the blood tests. When I was with him. He was still in a coma at the time, and they were rushing, there's a pressure to get it done quickly. They bullied his wife to sign a release form and they went for it. Of course, he was none the wiser, but he says he remembers a dream. He thinks he remembers a dream. He was in his house. It was dark, but he could tell he was at home. Everything was exactly right, exactly perfect, but he couldn't get any of the lights to work. He could find his way around, just about. And then he said he could sense this thing, this thing started to follow him, room to room. And he couldn't see it, but he could feel it, this intruder, this shadow. And something about it, something about how it moved, made it dangerous, made him scared. And he ran and he hid but it always found him. And when he woke up they told him that they had taken his blood. That intruder, it was us.

Beat.

And instead of his family being there, when he woke, it was a police officer, and his brother. And the police officer asked him if he remembered what happened, and he said yes, and if he knew where he was, and he said yes. And before he could ask where his family was, the officer explained that they had found alcohol in his bloodstream, and that he was under arrest. And so he realised why his family wasn't there, and why his brother looked like he did. Drinking. He was a devout Muslim, Tom, and he just got outed as a drinker by a police officer in a hospital.

Beat.

It was a bit later before they started asking him questions about terrorism. They asked him whether he was a member of any fundamentalist groups, whether he had any anti-Western opinions. They told him they took his computer and you know what his first thought was? He worried about his kids being able to do their homework.

Tom   Are you asking me to be annoyed with the police for doing their job, Sophie? Wouldn't you want them to be asking those kinds of questions? I'm glad about that.

Sophie   It had nothing to do with /

Tom   / You know that now. You know that today because you've got it all in hindsight. But no one knew then. No one had a clue what had happened. It was madness. And it was fair of the police to cover every angle.

Sophie   Every angle? He was just a bus driver.

Tom   No, Sophie. We didn't know that then. And don't pretend you didn't think it too.

Sophie   He was never the villain in this, Tom. He was just a man not coping. Working every shift he could to pay back a loan he took earlier in the year to afford some time off for his bad heart. See, if you tell them you've got a bad heart then you'll never work the buses again. So he lied, and he got in debt. And he started taxiing in the evenings, bouncing on double shifts on the buses to a night shift in a minicab, all the while trying to pay off this debt, look after a family and keep his bad health quiet. He was in a trap, Tom. And whose fault was that?

Tom   A lot of people have a shit time and they don't put lives at risk. No one dies because the man down the road loses his job, no one dies because a couple split up over failed IVF. The homeless don't go around fucking killing people. This isn't a kind or gentle world, Sophie. It's tough. And it's bleak. For everyone. What we don't need is someone coming here and making it harder.

Sophie   He fucked up. And he paid for that. He lost everything, Tom. His family, his house, he barely survived prison.

Tom   Oh, I'm sorry prison wasn't a comfortable experience for him.

Sophie   And he came out to a world that didn't want him, that at best thought that he was a drunken child killer, and at worst thought that he meant to do it. There isn't a second in the day where he doesn't regret his choices. So this, forgiveness, it isn't about taking that away, writing off what happened. It's about giving him some peace. We can end his punishment. For a second, for a moment, we can offer him some relief. Regardless of what happened, we can do that for another person. Isn't that a good thing in the world that you'd want George to see?

Tom   But why him? Why not someone that deserves it?

Sophie   Because I think we all do. Deep down.

Tom   Everyone?

Sophie   Yes.

Beat.

Tom   No.

Sophie   What?

Tom   You don't believe that. Be honest with me now, Sophie. If that driver had been white or whatever, would you be here now?

Sophie   What?

Tom   If the driver had been white, and I said in my statement that I thought I smelled booze. And I was proven to be right, would you have doubted me, would you have resented me, would you have split up with me, and would you now, four years later, be on my doorstep and try and guilt me into forgiving him? I don't think you would. This had nothing to do with the fact he was a Muslim for me, Sophie. He was a drunk, that's all people cared about.

Sophie   How can you say that, with the marches, the protestors, the threats to the hospital?

Tom   They weren't all against him, Sophie. I seem to remember a lot of people there too, demanding justice for him. For him!

Sophie   They wanted a fair trial. They thought, and were right to think, that the inquiry stitched him up. A space was created, a space between due process and the chaos of how it played out. And in that space he was made out to be a monster by xenophobes and racists and /

Tom   / How can you say that?

Sophie   And the papers did their best to keep it going. Speculation over cover ups and double standards for Muslim drivers. Claims that only white drivers get breathalysed, that foreign drivers were being shipped in from abroad and on dodgy licenses. And you were the one witness to speak the truth. You were the one that dared to call it what it was. That's what they said. And us, the never explicit but always implied, accusation that the rest of us survivors were lying.

Tom   I wasn't in control of any of that.

Sophie   But you were aware of it. And you resented the rest of us for not feeling the same way about you.

Tom   No.

Sophie   And maybe part of you, a bit of you, believed them when they said that the rest of us should have done more.

Tom   No. Of course not.

Sophie   Here you were. You were helping the police. You were being called a hero in the press. And us. Me, Carol, Roy, Mark and Sally, in our silence, you felt, were doubting you.

Tom   Did I feel on my own? Yes. Did I resent you for it? No. I didn't. I, I . . . You were going through whatever you were going through. That's none of my business. And as far as those groups are concerned. I condemned all that. I was explicit.

Sophie   Only once it was too late. Only once it had gathered a life of its own and you couldn't keep up with it anymore. I can see how at the start it made sense. It was a confusing, scary time. But you've got to realise that the people championing you, the people egging you on, were racist.

Tom   I don't know everything about each and every individual person who reads about me in the paper. So what if someone's racist? That doesn't make what happened in that inquiry racist.

Sophie   People were after blood and you made a judgement that that was ok. You used their energy. The prosecution used their energy. They didn't have to be in the room to make it impossible for there to be any other conclusion apart from it being entirely that man's fault.

Tom   Well you know what, there are some things they got right. Some things they got right.

Sophie   Like what?

Beat.

Like what, Tom?

Tom   You know, there's a difference between what the law says and what some nutter says. You can't seriously think that they . . . None of their shit, none of that shit can be left at my door.

Sophie   No?

Tom   No, Sophie.

Sophie   Some group posts on Facebook, a little quote, a picture of you. You can't blame people for making the link.

Tom   No one thinks that, no one is saying that.

Sophie   Well maybe not to your face.

Tom   What do you mean by that?

Sophie   Some loudmouth weirdo says something in public, doesn't even have to mention you by name, and someone will know, someone will remember. Someone somewhere will know it's you. And they're going to make the link. And whatever they think about them, they're going to think about you too.

Tom   No one's doing that. No one's, it's all in your head, Sophie.

Sophie   They might not say it to your face. But they'll think it. If I recognised you, if you moved in next door to me and I recognised you, I might not say it to you, but I'd say it to others.

Tom   *Someone, others, they* . . . Who are all these people, Sophie?

Sophie *looks out the window.*

Sophie   How do you know what they think in that café? When you go in, what they call you, what they talk about.

Tom   So they all meet in the café, do they? To talk about me?

Sophie   Something like that, a reputation like that, it can ruin you.

Tom   Ruin me? Is that what you're here to do?

Sophie   No, I /

Tom   / Because I tell you, Sophie. My life has already been ruined. Or what, now that I'm back on my feet, you're coming for more? Am I not allowed to move on?

Sophie   I'm not saying that /

Tom   / What about all the hassle I got? What about the reporters in my bins, at my mum's flat? They came for me too, and I did nothing wrong. You left me, the others left me. I was out on my own. They fucking tell me to do the right thing and then they drop me, do nothing to protect me when all your lot came for me. No one cared about me, no one, apart from . . . You know, I had to quit my job? Did you know that? Gary called me into the office and he said, *Look.* He said *we're getting too much attention here. I've got boys on the yard complaining that they don't feel safe, that they can't get on with their work.* Now, they couldn't sack me. Of course they couldn't. But he asked me to leave, and the way I saw it, I couldn't say no. None of you lot got fucking driven out of your work, had to move towns, had to start again. You know why I do this shit, flogging fucking tat on Amazon? Because I can do it in peace. Because I don't have people asking me who I am. And you come here and you start threatening, with /

Sophie   / No. I'm sorry. I just, I just got angry, with what they did to us, what they did to you. They manipulated /

Tom   / So I'm there, a year later, in this fucking shitty little bedsit above a chicken shop. I had no money, no job, no mates. My fucking mum's shit scared of the doorbell and I can't get up to help her because, never mind being skint, I can't get on a fucking road. And all I can do, all I'm doing is going over and over and over what happened that day. Hearing the cars beeping and revving outside my window. I can't get to the Job Centre because it's miles away and they don't understand on the phone why I can't get a bus. And so I get sanctioned, and I get cold, and I go hungry, and all the while I'm thinking of that driver there, his three meals a day and his bed and his fucking Open University courses and that in five years he'll be back on his feet.

Sophie   Well, for what it's worth, he never did get back on his feet.

Tom   Good. Because I did. And that's justice.

Pause.

Sophie   I never thought it was easy for you, Tom.

Tom   I know.

Sophie   And I don't blame you. For doing what you did. I was lucky, I think, the rest of us were lucky, that we were never put in that position.

Beat.

I didn't mean to leave you on your own.

Tom   And I didn't . . . I didn't mean either to, to lose you. To push you away like I did. With the booze and . . .

Beat.

Sophie   We never stood a chance.

Tom   I should have been there for you.

Sophie   Why didn't you talk to me?

Beat.

Tom   You left some stuff at my flat. Just a couple of tops and that. A book. I didn't realise until I moved, until I got the bedsit. I didn't know what to do with it. I'm sorry.

Sophie   Don't worry. I'd have probably just chucked it myself. I went through a stage of throwing everything away. I don't know. Like a kid. Just tearing everything . . . You did me a favour.

Tom   It's not been easy for you either.

Sophie   No. Well, you can say that.

Tom   And so I get it. I know why you're here. You come all this way. Knock on my door. It takes courage, Sophie. Don't get be wrong. You think forgiving him, getting me to forgive him, will be the thing that breaks the cycle. Helps you move on, rebuild, get out of the rut you're in. But it won't. It needs to be from you, it needs to be something inside.

Sophie   I'm getting there, Tom.

Tom   Tell me. How did you feel when you read that letter? Honestly, was it relief? Relief that someone needed you?

Beat.

Because I know how that feels. Here's my chance to prove myself, here's my chance to be important again.

Beat.

He never asked for this. Did he?

Sophie   Tom, I /

Tom   / He thought we were still together, right?

Sophie   Yes.

Tom   And so he thought, when he got in touch with you, he was getting in touch with the both of us. Right?

Beat.

He never asked you to hunt down a man that you hadn't spoken to in years. To track down his address, to find him in a different town and knock on his door.

Sophie   Tom.

Tom   Did he? Did he, Sophie? None of this is for him. It's for you.

The phone starts ringing again.

Sophie *starts to gather her things.*

Sophie   I should go.

Tom   No, don't. I want to . . .

Tom *answers.*

(*On phone.*) Hello? Yes, hi love. Oh right, ok. Well, I'm actually in the middle of something. Can I join you after? Yeah. Won't be long. Ta-ra.

Tom *hangs up.*

Beat.

They're going to the café. Good job we didn't, hey?

Sophie   Tom.

Tom   Listen.

Sophie   It was a mistake, coming here. It was a bad idea. It was a . . . I should have known. I'm sorry I disturbed you.

Tom *steps in front of the door.*

Tom   Now hang on. You can't do that, Sophie. You can't do this and then just go. That's not good enough.

Beat.

I thought about you.

Sophie   Tom.

Tom   Worried about you. Actually. Always at the back of my head, what, what . . . I wondered if you got out, if you'd . . . Why did you come here?

Sophie   To ask you /

Tom   / No.

Sophie   Because he wrote to me and asked /

Tom   / No, Sophie. Not him. What do you want from me?

Pause.

Sophie   I wanted to see if you did it. If you were able to, if you escaped. And the moment you answered the door, I saw it. I realised that yes, you had. All this. It's a different world.

Tom   I've changed.

Sophie   I know.

Tom   But I'm still /

Sophie   / How?

Tom   What?

Sophie   How did you do it? Why can't I? Why can't I move on like this?

Tom   Because you don't know the way out. You don't know your purpose.

Sophie   The thing that haunts me the most, the thing I can't get over, is why it was me and not them. All those lives, those futures. Kids, Tom. Why am I still here and they're not? What am I meant to do? It doesn't make any sense.

Tom   It does.

Sophie   Maybe for you. You've got George.

Tom   But I didn't. For a long time, I was like you are now. For a long time I was asking why. I'm a useless fucking, I wasn't going to change the world, I wasn't going to save any lives, I was a layabout fucking waste of space. But that, all that thinking, it's a symptom. I saw it the moment you turned up. You're sick. We all are. Until we're not.

Beat.

I was hiding, for a long time. Sat in that room. Busy places, people. I couldn't handle it. My hands would shake, I'd feel sick. I wasn't in control. I was ashamed. The guilt sat on me like this big blanket of concrete. I started to think that the people who died had had it easier than us. What the fuck is that? Thinking that I'd rather . . . And if I hadn't have found . . . If I didn't have someone to speak to, someone who listened to me, then I don't know what I'd have done. There are very few people who understand what we've been through. But they're out there. And they know that you can't do it on your own. They want to help, they want to support. The key word is support.

Beat.

And I'm not saying this to you now because I've got it perfect. Far from it. Claire's had to suffer, George suffers, and that's because of what I suffered. But it's useful for you to hear, because it does get better. With the right help, it gets so much better.

Sophie   How?

Tom   I was drinking. I was annihilating myself. If I could
have got out of my head quicker by cracking it open then
maybe I'd have tried, I don't know. I felt worthless,
ashamed. And if you feel like that for long enough then it
has an effect on you. You get smaller. You get weaker. Then
one day, I'm sat in this pub after getting my dole. And I'm
just going for it, caning it. And this man comes up to my
table. I remember his hand. I remember him stood there,
arm out, and he said *I want to shake your fucking hand, son*.
And he gripped it, and he said, *you, you know, you get it*. And I
thought, *know what, get what, you daft bastard*. And he told me
that I was a hero. And he bought me a pint. And he spoke to
me. And he opened my eyes.

Beat.

Guilt is a weapon used to put pressure on you. You forgave
that man straight away, Sophie. Why? Why do you have to
do that? What if you didn't? What if you allowed yourself to
be angry? You're allowed to be angry, Sophie. They want
you to shut up, to swallow it. You've done exactly what they
wanted you to do and it hasn't worked. Do you know what
happened to us that day, Sophie? Do you know what it was?
It was a failure. We were failed. Your country is defined,
historically, by one thing. By how it defends itself, by how it
protects its people. We weren't defended, we weren't
protected. Without the safety of its men, women and
children, a country is nothing, it's nothing. And it takes
moments like that, events like that, for us to really see the
truth.

The phone starts ringing.

Tom *looks at it.*

Sophie   Tom, what are you talking about?

Tom   You can only tell how strong something is by
observing how it responds to shock. All this talk, all this

endless fucking talk. It's useless. Where were our politicians when my arm was being wrenched from its socket? Who was there to mop up the blood of those children? Because it wasn't the fucking Prime Minister, it wasn't the Imams or journalists. That day, we saw how weak our country was. And it fucking crumbled. And they couldn't pretend that they were in control. What do you pay your taxes for, Sophie? What does it say on your passport? British citizen. You're allowed to be angry. After what happened to us, you should be. And if you see it like that, then you can see how all that violence, all that suffering, all that loss, means something. It exposes a truth. It makes madness make sense.

The phone starts ringing again.

You know, I think about it every day. I think about it every single morning when I wake up with George. And I'm thankful. Because I know what this world is, what it needs. The best decision I ever made was to get on that bus, Sophie. We went through something extraordinary. And it's our duty now to make sure that those losses weren't in vain, that the fallen died for a purpose. We're at war. Not with them. But with those that want to stop us from fighting back. See, I'm not talking about Muslims or, or . . . It's bigger than that. More important than that. There'll always be, you know, the history of our people is a history of war. That's never going to stop. But what has stopped, what doesn't exist anymore, is an army, is a belief that we can defend ourselves. And one day, people will realise. When the last bus has ploughed its way into pedestrians, when the last bomb has taken the roof off a shopping centre and when the last innocent person has opened their eyes, they're going to come to us, and they're going to ask us, to take back control. And my question for you, Sophie, is are you ready for that?

Sophie *breathes.*

End.

www.ingramcontent.com/pod-product-compliance
Ingram Content Group UK Ltd.
Pitfield, Milton Keynes, MK11 3LW, UK
UKHW020707280225
455688UK00012B/301

9 781350 087828